Frog. Frog? Frog!

Understanding Sentence Types

by
Nancy Loewen

illustrated by
Merrill Rainey

PICTURE WINDOW BOOKS
a capstone imprint

Before you start reading this story, there's something you should know. This is no ordinary family. Each person uses only one kind of sentence.

Interro (Dad)
Uses interrogative sentences only; he's always asking questions

Imperatella (Mom)
Uses imperative sentences only; she's always giving commands

Exclamuel (Brother)
Uses exclamatory sentences only; he's always showing strong feelings

DeClara (Sister)
Uses declarative sentences only; she's always making statements

Are you ready?
Turn the page.

3

"Do tell," said Imperatella.
"Don't be shy."

5

"DeClara caught a frog and it hopped into the

potato salad and into the pie and then it

jumped into Aunt Abby's hair and then it

dropped into the lemonade and Uncle Roly

got it out but he tripped over the

dog and the frog jumped down Granny Gail's

dress and she danced like a chicken!"

"Did you catch all that?" Interro asked.

"Slow down," ordered Imperatella.
"Start from the beginning."

"DeClara caught a frog!" Exclamuel said.

"That's correct," DeClara agreed. "I caught a frog."

8

"The frog hopped onto the picnic table! Then it hopped into the potato salad!" Exclamuel said.

"What happened then?" asked Interro.

"It jumped out!" Exclamuel exclaimed. "It landed in the pie!"

"What kind of pie was it?" Interro asked.

"It was peach pie," said DeClara.

"Don't stop now. Keep going," Imperatella urged.

"Aunt Abby tried to get the frog out of the pie," DeClara said, "but it jumped onto her head."

"What did Aunt Abby do then?" asked Interro.

"She said, 'jiminy cricket!' and shook her head like this!" said Exclamuel.

"Then the frog plopped into the pitcher of lemonade," DeClara said. "Everyone hollered. Except for me."

15

"How did you get the frog out of the lemonade?" Interro wondered.

"Uncle Roly grabbed the spoon from the potato salad and fished out the frog," DeClara said. "But then he tripped over Buddy."

"That's when the frog jumped down Granny Gail's dress!" Exclamuel said.

"Granny Gail flapped her arms and spun around and danced like a chicken," DeClara added.

"It was amazing!" Exclamuel exclaimed. "Hilarious!"

"It was hilarious," said DeClara.

"Where did the frog end up?" Interro asked.

Exclamuel threw up his hands. "I don't know!"

"I do," said DeClara.

About Sentence Types

What do we do when we talk or write? We make statements. We ask questions. We tell people what to do. And we show our feelings.

There are four basic kinds of sentences: declarative, interrogative, imperative, and exclamatory.

Declarative

Declarative sentences lay it out on the table, no questions asked. They state, tell, and announce. Declarative sentences end in periods.

Interrogative

Interrogative sentences need answers. They're curious. They quiz, probe, and wonder. Sometimes, like a lawyer on a TV show, they interrogate. Can you guess what kind of punctuation mark interrogative sentences end in?

Imperative

Imperative sentences tell people what to do. They instruct, order, and direct. Unlike other sentences, they can use two kinds of end punctuation marks: periods and exclamation points. They also contain an invisible word. That word is *you*. In a sentence like "Give Aunt Betty a kiss," the subject is understood to be "you," even if the word doesn't appear. "You give Aunt Betty a kiss" is the actual structure of the sentence.

Exclamatory

Exclamatory sentences are excited. Or maybe they're mad, surprised, or scared. They shout, cry, beg, and bellow. They get a lot of attention. Exclamatory sentences end in exclamation points.

Now you know all about sentence types. You do! What do you want to learn about next? Tell me.

Read More

Ganeri, Anita. *Grouping Words: Sentences.* Getting to Grips with Grammar. Chicago: Heinemann Library, 2012.

Prokos, Anna. *Track Star Sentences.* Grammar All-Stars: Writing Tools. Pleasantville, N.Y.: Gareth Stevens Pub., 2010.

Truss, Lynne. *Twenty-Odd Ducks: Why, Every Punctuation Mark Counts!* New York: G.P. Putnam's Sons, 2008.

Internet Sites

FactHound offers a safe, fun way to find Internet sites related to this book. All of the sites on FactHound have been researched by our staff.

Here's all you do:

Visit *www.facthound.com*

Type in this code: 9781404883215

Special thanks to our adviser, Terry Flaherty, PhD, Professor of English, Minnesota State University, Mankato, for his expertise.

Editor: Jill Kalz
Designer: Lori Bye
Art Director: Nathan Gassman
Production Specialist: Kathy McColley
The illustrations in this book were created digitally.

Picture Window Books are published by Capstone,
1710 Roe Crest Drive, North Mankato, Minnesota 56003
www.capstonepub.com

Library of Congress Cataloging-in-Publication Data
Loewen, Nancy, 1964–
 Frog. Frog? Frog! : Understanding sentence types / By Nancy Loewen.
    pages cm.—(Nonfiction picture books. Language on the loose.)
 Summary: "Introduces the four basic types of sentences—declarative, exclamatory, imperative, interrogative—through the telling of an original story"—Provided by publisher.
 ISBN 978-1-4048-8321-5 (library binding)
 ISBN 978-1-4795-1920-0 (paperback)
 ISBN 978-1-4795-1907-1 (eBook PDF)
1. English language—Sentences—Juvenile literature. 2. English language—Grammar—Juvenile literature. I. Title.

PE1439.L55 2014
428.2—dc23   2013008077

 Printed in the United States of America
 in North Mankato, Minnesota.
 032013   007223CGF13

Check out projects, games and lots more at
www.capstonekids.com

Look for all the books in the series:

Frog. Frog? Frog!
Understanding Sentence Types

Monsters Can Mosey
Understanding Shades of Meaning

whatever says mark
Knowing and Using Punctuation

When and Why Did the Horse Fly?
Knowing and Using Question Words